Praise for *The Savage Coloniser*

T0033442

'This stunner of a collection explores the savage iı
and before us in a way I haven't yet read articulated to this degree, with
this much poetic aplomb. Like a handbook it offers a poetic guide to
colonisation past, present and future, outside, within and beyond us.
Avia's poetic seer's eye . . . holds the dark up to the light to heal our
wounds.' —Selina Tusitala Marsh, *Academy of New Zealand Literature*

'A welcome autopsy of colonisers in past and present times, penned with
a scalpel's precision, the inspection of parts, minced down to the floor.
Sit in your blood-splattered apron and feel as the verdict is read.'
—Ali Cobby Eckermann

'With exquisite poise in every aspect of its poetic execution, *The
Savage Coloniser Book* is a torch that sets alight hundreds of years of
racist kindling that has been gathering under the oppressive yoke of
colonisation . . . and lets it burn.' —Leilani Tamu, *Kete Books*

'Tusiata Avia is one of the very best. *The Savage Coloniser Book* is about
colonisation: past, present and future. It's a book that expresses pain,
and anger, and it shows us the impact of history on the present:
sometimes by flipping situations around, and making us think – what
would happen if?' —Claire Mabey, *The Spinoff*

'*The Savage Coloniser Book* is a challenge and a gift. The thing above me
that I always thought was the sky has been revealed to be a roof, and
Avia has lifted it off me.' —Elizabeth Heritage, *Stuff*

'Tusiata Avia places herself – her ravaged heart, her experience, wounds,
scars, thinking, feeling, her urge to speak, sing, perform, make poetry,
no matter the price . . . – in her poems, in these necessary poems.'
—Paula Green, *NZ Poetry Shelf*

'Tusiata Avia's fourth collection is an astute and powerful postcolonial
poetic sequence. The forty-one poems here confront colonial history
with force and aplomb.' —Siobhan Harvey, *Landfall Review Online*

TUSIATA AVIA

Big Fat Brown Bitch

TE HERENGA WAKA
UNIVERSITY PRESS

Te Herenga Waka University Press
Victoria University of Wellington
PO Box 600 Wellington
teherengawakapress.co.nz

ISBN 9781776921294

A catalogue record is available from the National Library
of New Zealand.

Printed in Singapore by Markono Print Media Pte Ltd

Contents

1. Werewolf

2. The Big Fat Brown Bitch Jumps Over the Lazy Dog

3. Miracles

4. Malu | Protection

No white people were harmed in the making of this book

1

Werewolf

The author of The Savage Coloniser has hit back at ACT after the party called her work "hate-fuelled" and "racist". A stage show, which is receiving taxpayer money via Creative NZ, is now being produced based on the book by Ockham-winning poet Tusiata Avia.

ACT put out a press release criticising the book and stage show on Wednesday, saying the Government is "funding hate" with a show about "murdering James Cook, his descendants and white men like [him] with pig hunting knives".

"The Government, through Creative New Zealand, which taxpayers fund and whose board Ministers appoint, is supporting works that incite racially motivated violence," ACT leader David Seymour said in a statement on Wednesday morning.

... Seymour said the Government should come out and denounce the show and "declare it will give nothing to racism, and withdraw the funding".

"The Government says it wants to stop hate and then it appoints board members who fund this stuff. How is it any different from the kind of hatred that led to the Christchurch shootings?"

The Human Rights Commission told Newshub they have received complaints and queries in connection with published excerpts of 'The Savage Coloniser', which they're in the process of considering.

"We are precluded from making any specific public comments on the issues raised while we assess and respond to these complaints and queries."

Free speech poem

James,

the white,
in ▮ big *Endeavour*
sailing the blue, blue water.

James,

the
white

white.

James,
us

white men

descendants

incarnations.

We

full of

Justice

Resolution
Friendship
Discovery.

James,

god

and

king

New Zealand Media Council Complaints Case 3392

Sorry guys, the thing is, when I write a poem about colonisation I become a werewolf.

My views become exactly the same as those expressed in Germany. What I mean is, I'm the whole of Nazism and the entire Second World War.

When I write a poem about colonisation, sexual and racial violence burst out of me like wolf fur through the rents in my smooth brown skin. I start howling at the moon and inciting racial violence all over the place.

My daughter locks me in the bathroom and says through the door: 'Mum, stop that racist violence dressed up as art, because, Mum, poor white people disaffected by the effects of globalism couldn't say those things.'

My daughter slumps down outside the bathroom door in tears and whispers: 'I'm tired of my acceptable ethnicity. We brown people have all the privileges now. We can say anything we like and get away with it.'

<>

When I write a poem about colonisation under a full moon, I start writing hate speech and incitement to murder, which is exactly the same as the Christchurch massacrist's manifesto justifying the mosque shootings.

Exactly the same.

Now I'm howling and ripping off my clothes and writing a poem which is inciting violence right through the walls of my house.

The neighbours hear me writing a poem about colonisation and they yell: 'Stop that race-baiting, our kids are trying to sleep.'

Later, my white neighbour will come over to my house and say: 'Let me explain something to you, Tusiata. Racism is like a scab on your knee, and if you pick it, what will happen? Leave it alone and it will heal, otherwise I fear the wound will get infected. And what will happen to me then? Huh? What will happen to me?'

<>

When I write a poem about colonisation it turns into a hate crime right then and there. It springs up off the page and marches out into the street like ten thousand colonial soldiers armed with guns.

My poem steals my neighbour's land, and everybody's land. My poem steals 94 percent of all the land in New Zealand. It steals millions upon millions of acres of land.

My poem kidnaps children, puts them in state welfare institutions, abuses them and stops them speaking their own language. In the space of a few generations, my poem has traumatised the people who originally owned this land, and their language almost disappears.

My poem is no accident. My poem does all these things on purpose. My poem has a plan to take over everyone and everything.

<>

When I write a poem about colonisation, my moral compass is marginal at best and the consequences of my poem devastate innocent people all over the country. Look at my poem about colonisation, causing the radicalisation of people and ruining social cohesion.

Oh no! Here I go again, with my pen and my exercise book, inciting hate speech and dehumanising people.

Now, I want you to listen closely because I'm going to tell you something very important: Brown women are so privileged these days, we can get away with anything. If I was a white male I would be taken apart!

That's honestly how simple it is.

It is not complex.

No land theft. No genocide. No intergenerational trauma. No two centuries of white privilege.

There is truly nothing more to think about.

<>

Damn this poem! It is making my jaw grow long and shaggy. Fangs grow from my mouth and my eyes turn red. Here I go, on all fours now, with a tail growing out from under my skirt like a wild dog. Here I go, writing a racist rant about one of history's greatest explorers. How dare I!

Don't I know who Captain James Cook was?

Someone help me, please!

Because when I write a poem about colonisation, it is borderline terrorism.

Because when I write a poem about colonisation it is the same as an Isis beheading video.

<>

As I bound away, my daughter screams into the street behind me, 'Mum! I don't care how hard your upbringing was in Christchurch, it's just not fair that you get freedom of expression. I'm sick to death of us brown-skinned female poets and the generations of privilege we come from.'

Now the neighbours are out on the street, wringing their hands and shouting, 'Our children have access to this poem!'

Look at how the pendulum has swung. Things used to be in the right–white order. Things used to be fair. Things used to be normal. And now it's not safe to be white.

But it's too late. I am running with my Evil Brown Woman Poet Werewolf strength.

I am writing a poem which bursts into flames.

I am writing a poem which will burn down New Zealand.

I am writing a poem which will destroy the whole of Western civilisation.

Big Fat Brown Bitch 1: She is on the cross

The Big Fat Brown Bitch
Isn't nailed, she is strapped
It could be kink
Or kindness
Either way she is safe
Safe as a loving father
Sexy as a threesome
Enduring as heaven, earth and all creation
There is nothing ugly or terrifying
No jutting ribs or dripping wound that hurts us to look at
No painful emaciation
Nobody fingering her bleeding hole
She is big and fat and brown
And that strapping is clever and sexy as stripper shoes
Ahhh her wrists
And oooo her chunky ankles
Her chest is naked and her susu are big
Her loins are wrapped in siapo
Her look is all passion
No agony
There is enough of that on the ground, with the mourners –
Mary, all the Marys
The slutty one
The motherly one
The contrary one
The queen
The queer
The virgin
All the women looking up, waiting for her resurrection.

Hey David,

Aww, babe, are you OK?
I heard you read a poem today.
Oh no!

It's awful, ay?
That feeling you get when someone says something that upsets you.
Bae, I've been thinking about these lines of whakapapa behind us

long lines of ancestors, tripping over one another –
nanas and poppas, uncles and aunties shaking their heads
and throwing their tokotoko down in disappointment.

Hang on, bae, just listen for a minute.
Can you hear that still, small voice?

What are you doing, boy? Stop being stupid. Go inside and peel some spuds for Nanny
and don't you come out till you learn where your manawa is.

Hang on a minute, bae,
didn't you just say you were worried about the power of the state?
Y'know, like the majority silencing unpopular views?
Y'know what I mean, ay, bae?

Those hate speech laws that you said you're against?
Cos they suppress free speech, ay?
Like, umm, who are those guys you mentioned?

Mao Zedong and Adolf Hitler, ay?
Bae, if you're against that hate speech law, then won't 'hate speech'

– I'm putting quotation marks around those two words, bub,
so you know what tone I'm using here, OK? –

Won't 'hate speech' become too subjective and open to being abused?
That's pretty much, what *you* said, ay?
Gosh, you're clever!

But, cuz, as two people of Polynesian heritage, I really feel for you
cos, heck yeah, I can tell you from personal experience,
it really hurts when people hate you cos of the colour of your skin.

Cuzzy, it makes me really angry too.
I get so upset, that I have to go somewhere, sit down and write poems.
But the thing is, bub, they're only poems, ay?

And everyone – even my wee girl – knows what poems are like:
they're like storytelling, but with layer on top of layer on top of layer
of meaning
like umm

like a massive-massive layer cake
or a lasagne
or the layers of atmosphere protecting our planet.

They're like soul language.

Poems are awesome, bae, you don't need to freak out
and get hurt and angry and manipulative
and greedy for attention.

Calm down, bub.

Here, hold my hand, bae, it's OK
cos poems:
sometimes they like to make us feel

sometimes they like to flip the script
and make us wonder:
What would it be like if things were different?
And some poems, they can make us ask:
Why?

Keep reading. I'm nearly finished.
Yeah, I know, bub, it's a long time to listen
and not get to say anything, ay?

Poems do that too.

And for their next trick

They are doing an OIA on me.
OIA sounds like a shorter form of 'auoi' or 'auoia' –
an expression of shock or a cry in Samoan.

In English it means Official Information Act,
in Aotearoa it means this political party
intends to hold the government

(really? The whole government?) accountable
for anything mentioning my name, the name of my book
and the name of my play –

Tusiata Avia
The Savage Coloniser Book
The Savage Coloniser Show –

any email
text message
WhatsApp message

etc. that the 'government' might have.
There are screeds and screeds of me
and there is someone whose job, hour upon hour,

is to find me.
All of the 300-odd complaints
to the Race Relations Commissioner,
every other agency, department,

crown entity, organisation
and pubic hair subject to the Act.
I am large, I contain multitudes.

Do I contradict myself?
Ah, I have been reading ACT's
Protect Free Speech petition

Hear ye,
    It is minorities
    who need the protection of free speech

except when it is a poem
twisted into a headline
in an election year,

OIA, auoi, auoia.

Hate-fuelled racist

She is a hate-fuelled racist!
She is a hate-fuelled racist! She
She
She
She is a hate-fuelled racist –

Listen. It is you who is the hate-fuelled racist,
and you, a hate-fuelled racist,
and you,
and you,
and you are the hate-fuelled racists.

I am a hate-fuelled racist?
No!
I am not a hate-fuelled racist!
I am not
I am not
I am not a hate-fuelled racist!

And listen to this:
Cook was a hate-fuelled racist, too.

What? Cook?
No!
No!
No!
He was not a hate-fuelled racist!

She is the hate-fuelled racist.
Yes, that's right, HER,
SHE
SHE
She is the hate-fuelled racist.

Diary of a death threat,
15 March 2023 (Anniversary)

I went to Al Noor to remember.
To say sorry with lilies, the flowers for death,
white for peace, pink for the hearts stopped beating.

I don't know what I brought in with me
but the mosque bit my feet
outside the entrance, at the place you shelve your shoes.

I pulled my pink sneakers off
and the mosque bit my feet,
held them in its jaws, the hard warning of a holy beast,

held my soft feet in its mouth like a safe animal does
and then, as if under threat,
bit down hard till my feet broke

like when the earthquakes came,
when Papatūānuku rose up
and snarled *NO!* at the city fathers

and snapped them off
at their marble ankles
so their white statue bodies lay face down

in the liquefaction,
as the teacher of the earth says
lie there and think about what you've done,

the murder and the rape,
the white-washing
of your land thefts.

Maybe my fall was a tiny payback –
the whakapapa of my coloniser blood
setting it off,

tripping the jagged jaws of a gin trap.
I apologise to you, Al Noor,
for the sins of my forefathers

who floated in to Lyttelton Harbour,
the *Randolph*, the *Cressy*, the *Sir George Seymour* and the *Charlotte Jane*.
They thought they owned everything

and everyone.
They have a piece of me too, Al Noor,
the Jameses and the Johns

floating in my blood like so many fragments of their ships.
So, I will lie here with them, face-down in the mud,
and do my ifoga.

I will lie here with my broken feet
and think about how I walk on this ground,
part coloniser, part colonised.

The brown and white manuhiri.
I will walk like a guest in the holy temple that is the ground.
I will walk with respect for the dead,

for the martyrs, the Māori,
dead in the battlefields and the pā
and their mothers' arms,

of Taranaki and Waikato and Hutt Valley
and Bay of Plenty and Bay of Islands,
for the Shuhada, dead in the mosques of Ōtautahi.

All the martyrs,
their bones in the mud of this land,
their wairua always sweeping,

always sweeping across this land.

Diary of a death threat,
20 April 2023

I dreamt I had a stalker, not an I-love-you stalker
but an I-hate-you stalker,
an I-want-you-dead stalker,

and it was during the Olympics,
then I woke and remembered:
Oh, that's right, this is real life, it's not the Olympics,

not the real Olympics with people running and jumping and swimming
but here in real life there *are* people carrying torches,
not the Olympic torch, and not people dressed in white pointy hoods

but people dressed as good Kiwis,
horrified, righteous, furious Kiwis
carrying their torches across the country

to the steps of the Human Rights Commission
and the New Zealand Media Council
and over the airwaves and online –

because
I am a racist
I am a terrorist

I am a brown-skinned woman and
I am an incitement to violence
because

If a white man tried that,
he would be dismembered
but me, look at me:

stalking through this life untouched,
then I remember, Oh, that's right:
this *is* real life and someone really *does* want me gone –

someone would prefer me to be silent or hurt or maybe even dead.
I'm too nervous to open the letter and read it,
so I let my family read it and tell me what they think they should.

<>

I wonder what words are in that letter.
Are they short words in short sentences, staccato
like a fast one-two jab, like seeing stars and reeling and falling

or like a machine gun piercing every part of my body at once?
Are the words long and sinuous, would they wrap themselves
around me and squeeze the breath out of my chest

and hot pain into my stomach? Would they rear up
and look at me, hypnotise me, bite me between the eyebrows,
shoot poison straight up into my brain?

Are the words dancing words,
spinning and spinning so fast, so fast
the whole world throws up?

When I explain to the police they say:
There's not much we can do
because if this man says, *That wasn't me,*

I didn't send that threat,
someone else used my name –
if he says that, there's nothing we can do.

< >

I wonder what would happen if my stalker
stood by his letter and said: *Yes, it was me, I used my own name.*
Admitted: *That is me. Yes, I want her gone.*

What would happen then?
Would we go to court?
Be together in a place I could see him clearly

and he could see me, as if we were on a date
but separated by people speaking for us.
Everything is a relationship.

Everything that happens,
happens inside a relationship.
I never hear from the police again.

Diary of a death threat,
1 May 2023

Deep down under the earth, past the sea,
the Samoan Goddess of War simmers,
waiting for my call. Wait. She will burst out

from the underground, all four battle clubs
spinning   spinning
like the whine of death approaching –

Really, bitches? I write a poem about Captain Cook
and you scurry around in your dark spiderweb,
in your pyjamas?

Really, bitches? I can hear the unclipped claws
on your teeny tiny paws
clicking   clicking

Do I hurt your feelings? Are the spiritual descendants
of Captain Cook and George Grey in pain today?
Is the land you're sitting on groaning in the wind?

Is a voice blowing under your doors
and the cracks in your windows?
Are you angry, baby?

And sending me death threats
for writing about what happened
and calling Captain Cook a bitch?

Baby, he was a bitch
And so were Grey and Rolleston and Hobson.
Here's what happened:

For stealing trillions of dollars worth of land
and raping the women and children
and murdering the men

and keeping on doing that
till today
to our babies

in your schools
and your prisons –
for doing all of that

the guilty received no punishment,
no consequences,
nothing.

I'm not even allowed to write poems about them
in case their descendants – by belief or blood –
get upset and feel

like someone hates them
or is being racist
towards them.

Baby, there are bitches
everywhere you look these days
and maybe, baby, you're a bitch too.

The past is the past

Culture aside, there comes a time when you people have to stop making excuses.

Racism aside, there comes a time when you are just being lazy and drunk and violent. It's the same as those Aborigines in Australia. But there are some good ones, just like there are some good Mour-rees over here.

History aside, why do they drink so much? Sure, I have a few drinks, but I know when to stop. And, sure, when I was at uni I used to get really drunk, but it was nothing like what you people do. I've seen it with my own eyes, I've been to Alice Springs.

You bring your problems on yourselves, I mean it's disgusting the way you people behave in public.

Culture aside, if I behaved like that, what would happen? Think about that. It's two different rules in this country. If you're a Mour-ree or even a Sim-mow-win you get special treatment. That's just a fact.

History aside, there comes a time when all that stuff is in the past and you people need to stop complaining. Waitangi this and Dawn Raids that – if everyone got an apology from the prime minister, I mean, where would it all end? It's not like I'm responsible for any of it! If you think about it, *I'm* probably owed an apology for something too.

What I'm saying is, the past is the past, so let's leave it there and just get on with it.

White privilege aside, my parents weren't rich and look at me – I still went to uni and got a good job. I work hard for my money and I'm proud that my kids go to private schools.

There comes a time where we've got to get tough and lock your kids up before they commit crime. Why are they ram-raiding?

Intergenerational trauma aside, those 14-year-olds and those 10-year-olds – military training is the answer. Teach them some consequences and some discipline. We would never have gotten away with that sort of thing.

Just look at them on the streets in those hoodies, the way they walk, like black people from those American gangsta movies.

That's why I cross the road when I see them coming.

That's why I tell my kids to cross the road when they see your kids coming.

Culture aside, there comes a time when you people just need to try harder and get off your bums and go to school and get proper jobs.

Big Fat Brown Bitch 23: She receives an election-year visit

If you are sitting in a garage in South Auckland with your two brothers, tell your sisters to stand outside on the street, flag down flash cars and check for gang members or members of parliament.

If you are sitting in a garage in South Auckland with your two brothers, hide your BA, MA, PhD and your MNZM for services to the arts, the sciences, sports, healthcare and technology. Think instead how you might get into a gang and a life of crime.

If you are sitting in South Auckland with your two brothers, writing an opera for SOL3 Mio or Isabella Moore or Pene Pati (the new Pavarotti), stop what you are doing and flag down a gang member and buy some meth. Make a real brown living, for God's sake!

If you are sitting in South Auckland with your two brothers, discussing the majestic architecture of atoms, the rhythm of the tides and the luminescence of the galaxies – shut that down immediately and consider the gang life and what it has to offer you.

If you are sitting in a garage in South Auckland with your two brothers and gang members or members of parliament, you're on the right career path, whichever gang you join.

If you are sitting in a garage in South Auckland with a certain member of parliament, keep him distracted with stories of your gang affiliations while your two brothers pick the lock and rifle through his BMW 7 Series for keys to any of his other luxury cars or houses or account numbers to any of his off- or on-shore accounts.

If you are sitting in South Auckland with the member of parliament and your daughter brings in cups of tea and coconut buns and bends to whisper in your ear *He's worth 30 million dollars, Mum,* tell her to hide the other kids in the wardrobe, under the bed and in the chest freezer, and keep him busy with a conversation about putting criminals aged 10 to 17 in bootcamps.

If you are sitting in a garage in South Auckland with the 2023 Prime-Minister-hopeful after he has put his racist foot in his mouth again, offer him a hi-vis vest so he can hammer in a few nails with your two brown brothers smiling in the background. Then see him off on his trip to Christchurch.

Hi guys, I am here at McDonald's Merivale and it's a very special place. I have a huge appreciation for the people, the Golden Arches, the Air NZ baggage handlers, the call centres, the apprentices. #Luxononthejob!

Macca girl's song

I will not make you burgers, sir
I will not
I will not serve your friends
burgers in warm, greedy boxes.

I will, though
serve them knife, machete, broadsword, switchblade
I hold all four in my hands
I know what I am doing.

So lie the fuck down
get on your front
listen to these four swords circle me
with my knee on the butterfly of your shoulder-blades.

Don't move or I swear
I will defy my own fear and cut you
I will slash you
here on the cheek

and the slide of your ribs
this short smooth blade
into the soft eye socket
of anyone who tries me

I will cut you
like my gym membership
like my diet plan
like feminine wash.

Glorious ways rap

Let me refer to myself in glorious ways
Let me refer to myself in these fucked-up days
I got a medal from the queen, enough awards around my neck
like Flava Flav but big and gold, enough to melt down and bedeck
golden grills for my teeth and nifo koula for the Tongans
I got Arts Laureate, Distinguished Alumni, I keep on goin'
Got a Fulbright, got Off-Broadway, got that Ockham
I can list them all day –
Winston, who you callin'
a 'mediocre poet'? Bro, you so irrelevant
and Aotearoa, we all know it
David Seymour, who you callin' racist?
you just some double-talking, weaponising, headline-grabber, face it!
Listen up:
How many girls you know write like this?
How many girls you know fight like this?
Cos here I am, bro
The way is narrow
I see you –
No real principles or ethics, just racist fear and white hysterics
You're here to win votes, rack up the bank notes
but you should take care, beware your eye-mote
Won't let you blind us with noxious whiteness
That's why I write plays (that's why my work slays)
Cos, I am the girl who writes like this
I am the girl who bites likes this
Yeah, here I am, bro
sharp like an arrow.

Spaceship for white people

I am not afraid.
I can speak that language.
You should hear me –

I'm unbelievable, I'm truly and absolutely believable, everything I say sounds like, *I have a big white expensive penis.* I can look into his white hair and his blue eyes and the white ceiling above me and he will hear me and for a moment not even notice the difference.

He is impressed with my enunciation
my elocution
my erudition
my acculturation
my complete and absolute codification.

He forgets who I am and who I look like and he treats me as an equal; he forgets who I am so much even I think I'm a white man.

I feel triumphant and satisfied and sovereign as Networks, as Old Boys, as Christ's College, Kings College, Cambridge.

But I am tired, tired of labouring in this language that elevates me.

<>

It's spaceshippy in here –

looking into the rich white light where seven white beings move around me, speaking in my language but not in my language at all.

It's white the way they look at me, the second whitest one saying, *You never know who they're letting into first class these days*

and the third one turning to me to say, *Don't worry about him, you are a credit to your race* and telling the others not to worry, they won't be needing the translation machine for this one at all.

<>

I am not afraid.
But eventually I leave.
I lie down. I weep into my own ears.
I am not afraid.
I am just
really
really
really
fucking tired.

Ode: Don't punish the wealthy

Oh, Nicola, I really don't have time for this today, I'm wiping the damp from the walls for God's sake, I'm feeding my babies instant noodles for God's sake, and you're telling us: *Don't punish the wealthy*, so, I just have to sit down for a minute and write a poem.

Because what else am I gonna do? When you and Chris and David say shit that makes us angry and powerless and stupefied, what else am I gonna do?

Compare you to Captain Cook? Call you bitch? Or David a bitch or Chris a bitch or Winston? What else am I gonna do?

Come for me, babe, what else have I got to lose?

Don't punish the wealthy.

Eat the poor.

We are big and fat these days, Nicola. The poor aren't skinny like you guys, we are fat from all the two-minute noodles (you'd be surprised at the fat content in those suckers) and the $1 loaves of bread here in South Auckland and Porirua and Aranui. Can't get Vogel's in our dairy, babe, and who's got money for that anyway, or petrol to get to the supermarket?

Don't punish the wealthy – whoever they are. I haven't actually met any of them. They don't come to our dairies or our garages or know our brown brothers who live in them, who y'all talk about like you've even met us. You know the reference I'm making here, ay, babe?

Eat the poor instead, Nicky, we are fat and juicy and our kids are full of phlegm, it's all the carbs and the cold. Yeah, even here in subtropical South Auckland, Nic, the walls are weeping and the bedrooms are cold.

Kids and their coughing are the ones you should punish, they're running this economy into the ground with their free doctors' visits, but don't worry: eat us. You know we have a cannibal past and you are vying for queen, and royalty always gets the choicest cuts – the back of the neck is the best bit – so let's get the BBQ going, the hāngi going, the umu going.

Lie us down and wrap us in the New Zealand flag, lie our mucus-filled babies down and wrap them in blue, which is also the Crips' colour.

You guys have lots in common – the Crips and the National Party – both of you train the hard way. The Crips train from babyhood, on the streets, like boot camps. National trains *our* babies in *their* boot camps. The profits, the rackets, the gang pride, the blue verses the red.

Don't punish the wealthy.

Eat the poor.

We will keep you going all day. The choice backs of our necks will power you through these hard times, this recession coming, the hard fight at the ballot box coming. We will keep you so warm you'll have to open your windows at night and breathe in the fragrant air of Epsom and Khandallah and Merivale.

Take a big bite of us, babe.

Don't punish the wealthy.

Eat the poor.

Dawn Raids Apology 2022

The princess of Tonga speaks to the prime minister and makes us cry

HRH Princess Mele Siu'ilikutapu Kalaniuvalu Fotofili
tells Prime Minister Ardern why we are crying.

MP Carmel Sepuloni blots her eyes
and we unleash our tears

like police dogs at dawn
on our father, his bare feet,

his hands cuffed behind his back,
his pyjamaed legs scrambling

into the back of the police van
while his babies scream.

Some of us hold our tears back
like our mother telling us

be quiet, quiet
in the dark,

dark
hiding places

of Auckland and Wellington
and Christchurch and Dunedin.

I accept your apology
Her Royal Highness says
and lowers her silver head and chuckles

HOWEVER...
the Vā
the Vā
the Vā

between the princess of Tonga
and the prime minister of New Zealand

is the space across the stage at the Auckland Town Hall
and the number of Tongan overstayers
still hiding from capture in 2022.

Polynesian Panther Alec Toleafoa raises his fist

Alec greets the government. This is rare, very rare.
Usually he is 16, 17, usually he is moe pī,
usually he is a bunch of upstarts,

usually he is *educate to liberate,*
usually he is a raised fist, a loud-hailer,

the running of panther paws
away from an MP's house at dawn
before the pigs arrive.

He raises his fist and he cries
What do we need?
Healing!

When do we need it?
Now!

MP David Seymour looks confused

David and the red-faced man sitting next to him are wondering
wondering wondering

when to stand and when to sit
what all the words are
what all the words are
why the women with the red feathers and mirrors on their heads
are walking backwards like that
why the Minister for Pacific Peoples has taken his shirt off
and why he is holding a fly whisk
and where the flies are coming from
and where the flies are going
who the men at the feet of that princess are
why those aggressive men are holding spears.
And why have they painted their faces black?
Surely that's not very PC these days?

David looks around at the never-ending sea of brown.

Reverend Tevita Finau delivers his sermon

Our reading today is from the Book of Dawn Raids,
chapter one, verses one to five:

*And in those days, the police of the Pharaoh Muldoon
drove through the highways and byways of the land called Ponsonby and Grey Lynn
where lived the sons and daughters of the great Pacific Ocean.*

And the police of the Pharaoh did play recordings of dogs barking
to send fear into the hearts of all those who had ears.
And out of the houses fled the overstayers.
The sons and daughters of the great Pacific Ocean
flew out of their houses and over the fences away from captivity.
But, alas, the police of the Pharaoh Muldoon were wicked
and had tricked the sons and daughters of the great Pacific Ocean
and lay waiting for them with large and hungry dogs who did indeed eat them.

Let us pray.
Dogs are used for chasing pigs.
Dogs are used to capture swine.
Dogs are not for the royal houses of
Tacombau of Fiji
Pomare of Rarotonga
Tupou of Tonga
or Tupua and Malietoa of Samoa.

Allow us to pass freely without hindrance.
We are not passing through like American tourists.
We are here like the British overstayers.

(Are they are so white as to be invisible?)

We are not leaving and we are tired, tired of waiting, waiting in the dark.
We await you, Prime Minister, to grant our people visas,
in the name of the Father, the Son and the Holy Ghost.

Āmene
Āmene.

Ifoga: Prime Minister Ardern is covered by the ceremonial fine mat

She is in white.
She sits on a chair.

The ie toga is spread over her head like a bridal veil,
the ie toga is spread over her body like the beloved.

This is not prostration,
this is not as long as it takes for the sun to rise and set again,

this is not more than a minute
(she has demanded not more than a minute).

This is not face down on the floor till we say you are forgiven
but she has calculated that this is more authentic
than Prime Minister Helen Clark standing at a microphone in 2002.

The mat is lifted
and the sins against our forefathers call,

our pearls who were cast before dogs call,
the tears of our princess call,

This is not the end.
This is just the beginning.

2

The Big Fat Brown Bitch Jumps Over the Lazy Dog

She goes to the hospital

It begins with the nurse measuring me – height and weight.
She leaves and returns, with a look on her face, and says
blah blah blah Body Mass Index
blah blah blah Do you know about food?
blah blah blah You big fat brown bitch.

She doesn't actually say, You big fat brown bitch.
But she means, You big fat brown bitch.

She also means: You big fat brown lazy bitch.
You big fat brown stupid bitch.
And: You big fat brown worthless bitch.

I don't tell her that I know the Body Mass Index
was invented by a man named Adolphe,
a white man measuring white men's bodies – the measure
of the social ideal
in 1830, boom time of racist science, genocide and colonisation.

I don't tell her that by the early 1900s the BMI became the rationale
for eugenics, for the sterilisation of the disabled,
the autistic, the poor and the coloured.
I don't tell her this because I know she can never believe
what exits the mouth of a big fat brown bitch.

So, I draw myself up to my full Big Fat Brown Bitch height
and try to look sure of myself, but not too threatening
educated, but not too threatening
and calm, but not too threatening.

Big Fat Brown Bitch 13: She was so grateful to be grateful to be grateful

I was grateful my name was Donna
when a teacher was calling a Māori name in roll call
or saying *Richard Too-a-tara* instead of Richard Tuatau
and then calling him a lizard and all the kids laughing

I was thankful my name was Donna.
Someone got wind of my middle name
and called me *Tissy-arse-wetter*
and everybody was laughing

and later, on the way home,
two boys stopped me in the street
and spat on me.
Spat on my blue school jersey –

first, one gob of pale hoik
landing somewhere near my heart,
then another, running down my chest
like filthy tears

and then those two boys laughed at me
and called me *Tissy-arse-wetter*
and *boonga* and *coconut* and *nigger*
and all I could do was listen to the drumming in my ears

and try to sneer a little bit.
It was enough being big and brown
and a girl in Christchurch in 1979.
I didn't need a weird name that no one could say.

I was grateful my name was Donna
every time I heard another brown kid's name
and every time a teacher called a kid, even if they were white,
a *mour-ree*, because it was another word for *idiot*.

Everyone said it then – *Don't be a Mour-ree*
just like we said *Don't be a Jew*
to the kids who wouldn't share their lunch
or their paper or pens or whatever it was we wanted,

even though none of us knew exactly what a Jew was.
I had seen pictures of them in Mum's World War Two books –
bodies tangled in heaps on the ground in Auschwitz and Belsen,
the scary skeletal faces peering out of the black and white stripes.

Sometimes I said silently to myself
Thank God my name is Donna and not Tusiata
when someone read *Donna* out again
and again and again and again,

when someone called my name
across the classroom
or the playground,
again and again and again.

Your name is the truest thing
that anyone ever calls you.
It's like the sound of your footsteps
through the echo-cave of your life.

I was grateful and thankful and relieved and grateful again
to the guardians of all English, normal-sounding names
that my name was Donna
and not Tusiata.

Now Donna lives somewhere just outside White Scar Caves in Yorkshire,
mostly silent and mostly still.
Every now and then I will hear her name
and my daughter will turn to me and laugh

like someone has called me Macaroni Eightyfive,
Batman bin Superman, Jesus Condom Clown Tricycle,
or Krystal Ball – like it's the most ridiculous name
anyone has ever been given.

Big Fat Brown Bitch 99: She jumps over the lazy dog

The Big Fat Brown Bitch jumps over the lazy dog.
The Big Fat Brown Bitch jumps over the crazy hospital
and the lazy school
and the hazy whakapapa
and the Jay-Z wannabe Kiwi male.
The white gaze says: *Jump, Big Fat Brown Bitch, jump.*
The Big Fat Brown Bitch jumps over the nasally store detective.
The Big Fat Brown Bitch jumps over and over
and pays and pays.
The Big Fat Brown Bitch jumps like rays of light
over the setting sun,
like rays from alien weapons
over the judgement of God,
the Big Fat Brown Bitch jumps over neo-Nazis
and white supremacists and David Seymour
and all the people who used to be brown
who hate anyone who could be them,
the Big Fat Brown Bitch jumps over tasers, and runs –
the Big Fat Brown Bitch, boy she can run
with a cop on her tail for no rego, no warrant of fitness
and four brown babies in the back seat,
the Big Fat Brown Bitch jumps this way and that way
every way and always –
see the Big Fat Brown Bitch run,
see the Big Fat Brown Bitch scream,
wee wee wee wee
all the way home.

Big Fat Brown Bitch 106: She wishes
she could jump over the lazy pig

The Big Fat Brown Bitch eats at the same time as she works
because she doesn't want to be a big fat lazy pig.
When she is lying in bed in the morning
without leaping up as if her feet are in the boiling pot
she is a lazy pig.
When she closes a file and opens Netflix
she is a lazy pig.
When she is still watching Netflix at 5 in the morning
she is a lazy pig.
When she wakes up in the morning or the afternoon
and can't open her eyes
she is a big fat lazy pig rolling in her own shit.
When she lets her teenage daughter get herself ready for school
she is a big fat bad mother lazy pig.
When she puts something in the microwave
she is a big fat stinking bad mother lazy pig.
When she orders food on Uber Eats
she is a big fat useless wasteful bad mother lazy pig.
When she talks on the phone
she is a lazy pig
unless it's a work call.
When she drinks coffee
she is a lazy pig
unless it's to keep her awake to do some more work.
She is a lazy pig when she's answering work emails
because she's still not strictly working-working.
She is a lazy pig when she is making dinner
or looking after her children
because that is not her proper work.

When her clothes don't fit
she is the fattest of all lazy pigs everywhere.
Falling over
or wanting to throw herself off a bridge
or down the stairs means
she is a crazy lazy pig.

She has a headache.
She wants to put her head out the window
and scream into the world: I am NOT
a Big Fat Brown Bitch fucken lazy pig,
and I have had enough.

But her headache means
she is a lazy pig.
Her osteoarthritis means
she is a lazy pig.
Her epilepsy means
she is a lazy pig.
Her crutches mean
she is a lazy pig.
Her wheelchair means
she is a lazy pig.
Her mobility scooter
means she is a lazy pig
and honestly the ugliest biggest fattest
laziest pig in the entire country.

Big Fat Brown Bitch 4: She loses weight

Look how skinny I am now!
Me looking at myself in shop windows,
me looking at myself in the whites
of the eyes of all the people who smile at me now,
me looking at myself in the whites
of the eyes of all the white men who see me now.
I run my hands over my slightly rounded size-12 stomach.

Me looking at the inside of my size-12 stomach,
the octopus squirting poison against the lining of my stomach,
me looking at myself under the MRI of the setting sun
shining through the honeycomb of my bones,
the arthritis of my knees and hips,
the chips out of my skull,
the fractures running like a river system,
the Nile,
the Blue Nile,
the Yangtze,
the filthy Avon.

See! See! screams my new body
see how skinny I am
see how broken I am
see what a miracle it is that I can walk without crumbling
that I can stand in the rain without my head filling up like a sieve
the coils of my brain snaking up like worms from the wet grass.

Big Fat Brown Bitch 5: She puts weight on again

See what a fucking miracle I am
I am a triumvirate
I am a trinity
My body is big enough for three women to share

A birthing woman is a goddess
I have the body of a birthing woman
One that constantly splits open to birth another bitch
What else splits open to reveal a whole new squalling universe?

Admire my big fat brown body, bitches!
Admire it!

Big Fat Brown Bitch 87: She feels most Samoan in a room full of white people

I feel even more Samoan in a room full of white people
interested in the fact that I'm   Samoan
like at a writers festival. Like on the stage
at a writers festival where everyone is   Samoan
or some other kind of 'diverse'
while everyone in the audience is the opposite of diverse

like in a bookshop when I know I'm being followed
(because what is she doing here?)
like I'm seventeen and one of school governors says,
So, tell me, what does it feel like to be   *Sim-mow-win?*
like I'm thirteen and we're studying Sāmoa
in social studies and Mr Adams says
Now everyone look at Donna   see the wide nose

I feel most white in a room full of Samoans speaking   Samoan
and ignoring me. I feel even more white
when they're laughing at me. I feel the whitest
when a man in   Sāmoa
says, *I thought you were a full pālagi*
See Tusiata   see her pālagi nose

I feel most afa kasi when white people call me *that big Mour-ree woman*
I feel most afa kasi when I have to see my family in   Sāmoa
I feel as half-caste as a donkey plus a horse equals a mule

Cast me like a colour or lack of a colour
Colour me in like I'm the colour brown or light brown or white

or black sometimes (when someone calls me a nigger).
White is a colour because one of our prime ministers said so.

Throw me like a colour against a canvas or the footpath
or an unmade bed or the eyes of a classroom
or a New Zealand literary festival or a lunchtime crowd
in a Wellington bookshop,
throw me like a colour and see what happens.

Another England built

When I google these streets I get two stabbings in one week
I get taxi drivers who refuse to come here

I get somebody's sleeping father up against the dryer in the laundromat
I get somebody's cross-legged grandfather begging outside the dairy.

When I google these streets I get the first stabbing
at the end of our street and the second stabbing at our shopping centre

outside the new parole office
which before it was a parole office

was the New World supermarket
which before it was the New World

was the family holiday caravan park
where Vicky, the English girl, lived with her English sister

and her English mother
who worked at the New World.

Down from there is the new super-school
which before it was a super-school

was Aranui Primary School
where Vicky and I went

and Wainoni and Avondale primary schools where my cousins went
and Aranui High School where we all went.

Now it's the place where all the kids from here are kept
in a great big massive super-school

which is only a short walk from the corrections centre
parole office

so the kids won't get lost.
So when our kids grow up, they will remember the way

from school
to corrections
to parole.

Easy.

Big Fat Brown Bitch 66:
She performs an exorcism

Hey! Spirit!
Spirit of spit in the faces of the ancestors

spirit of chase down the children
spirit of old murderers

spirit of the latest one –
Incubus!

Running for election
on our local school board –

Daemon!
Driving in your death van

plotting another massacre
playing it over and over

in the mind called Legion –
your fathers' fathers' fathers.

I call the bone dust of the dead
from the foundations

of these buildings, these houses
hospitals, prisons

and rugby stadiums
to rise and resurrect.

I walk across this city
and call,

Show yourself.
Show your goddamned self.

All the babies

She hid it in the bush
at the rubbish pile,

left it at the storage facility
in the shed.

A trench of girls,
still-bleeding girls.

A day off school
in loose clothes.

She never showed
or told.

Girls in school
who kept quiet,

very very quiet,
girls who never told,
who couldn't,

girls we can't,
just can't
imagine.

Memorial 2021

Christchurch, 22 February 2011

The quake families sit in rows and rows and rows.
We stand by them, we cuddle each other.
The flags flutter: Japan, Israel, Canada, UK, USA
and ones we'll have to google later.
We sit under the sky, no walls,
no roofs, we will be safe here.

The kaikaranga calls.
Jacinda walks the aisle like a bride in black.
Our hearts skip and our cameras shake –
red petals, black petals, dust and bone and concrete petals.

Karanga mai ra,
the dead are close,
they have come from Hawaiki Nui.
The grieving are the silent sea, the river Avon runs,
it trickles down our cheeks.

The waka has returned.
HNZM sits in the harbour of our moana,
as she sat there ten years ago.
All the sea is made of tears.
The Japanese families cannot be here,
we cry into our masks for them.

It was 20 seconds that changed us
20 seconds that killed us
185 dead

They say that if the building was built
to code, 95% of those who died there
would've survived.
Some of us know this
and it flips and flips
like the ika in the Avon
sick and struggling through the waters.

Yes, we are still sad
and tired and anxious
us and our kids.
My three-year-old is thirteen now.
She looks at me through eyes
of the rebuild generation,
the trauma generation.

Army bands make us cry
Speeches make us cry
95% makes us cry
Flags make us cry
Japan makes us cry
The women in wheelchairs make us cry
The turn to Oi Manawa makes us cry
The ship's bell makes us cry
12:51pm makes us cry

their names
their names
their names
their names
our tears clouding the sun.

3

Miracles

She's got her grandmother's bum

Last time she was here in New Zealand,
I was eight or nine or some other really impressionable age
when a string of words from the mouth of an adult could

float on the air like a malarial mosquito
and fly into my ear canal
and burrow into my brain to hatch its noisy young.

You've got your grandmother's bum.
Yes, you've got your grandmother's bum.

My sister used to laugh at my grandmother
behind her back
because her bum was big.

It was wide
and it swayed
not in a way we thought beautiful

but like a sinking ship,
like a ship in peril,
like a ship thrown up by the massive scary waves,

plunging down so fast that the screaming people
on board lost their footing,
flew up into the sky and drowned in the savage sea.

You've got your grandmother's bum.

Now I know she came here in nineteen seventy-something
to replace the hip that could no longer hold her level.

She pitched when she walked.
She limped when she walked.
She lurched and cast and heaved when she walked.

And because she was old-school Samoan
and even though she was in New Zealand
and even though it was pretty cold down there

she still sat cross-legged on our floor.
It took her the careful construction
of three pyramids to get up:

first, the turning of her waist,
then hands flat on the floor, to one side,
then the brace of her elbows –

the first triangle.
Then the lower body twist
and the hoist to her knees –
the second triangle.

Then feet flat, legs braced,
her head to the floor – her hips, her bum,
the flat top of the final pyramid.

I used to watch her
construct Giza many times a day.
Now, I do yoga
and I know the only way my grandmother

could get up off the floor
was to do downward dog.

It's the only way I can get up.

Now I have my grandmother's arthritic hip.
Now, I have my grandmother's bum.

Rest home poem

Don't leave me here, please
No, no, I have no control over it, Mum
You're just being mean
I'm not being mean, I told you Mum,
I've got to go, I'm late, just go back to your room
No, please, please, please
No, I'm going now.

When he was five he cried for her.
When he started school, he cried
and one of the boys put his arm around him
at play time. And when the bell rang at three o'clock
he went home and she was there.
She was always there.

Miracles

Some things in this life have to happen/ and I have to lose my foot/
I don't know why/ the danger of this whenua?/ punishment?/ I
don't know/ it's just as inevitable as cut and you will bleed/ whether
by your own hand/ another's/ deserved/ or not/

My right leg ends a couple of inches above the waist of my missing
ankle/ it is clean-cut like a mannequin missing her screw-on foot/
still in the store window still doing her job/ wearing her skirt and
her top/ doing her job/

Even mannequins need a break/ sitting with my legs under the
dining room table/ I could be a normal person/

When I look down/ there it is/ my foot growing back/

This is a miracle/ a miracle/
like the raising of the dead man/ *Look! Look!* I cry/

just like the sister cried when the dead man came back to life/

Look! I shout/ *See my Lazarus foot?/ Behold, it grows back/ Behold, the
appearance of the navicular, the metatarsal, the heel, the toes and the toe
nails sprouting from absolutely nowhere/ Behold/*

Later/ I miss the clean ending of my right leg/

I miss/

the simplicity of a life without miracles/

Recovery room

Afterwards I listen to them telling the man
on the other side of the curtain
that they have removed a tumour from his brain

I touch my own head
I touch my own head and thank it
Thank you for not having a tumour

and the floating woman beside me fills me with drugs
so many drugs

morphine
and fentanyl
and the one that killed Michael Jackson

Don't worry, she says, *it's only a bit of fun*

Commode

I hate the commode.
It is a thing meant to be hidden
under the whiffy skirts of Victorian matrons
or further back – the reeking Elizabethan ones,
when no one washed at all.

At first glance the commode
reads as a chair or a wheelchair – a helpful thing –
but then the shocking yawn,
the open hole,
the open pit

that might appear anywhere –
the bedroom, the hallway, the kitchen even.
The offence of it, the foul of it.
The way you now have to use it as a wheelchair
but with no push-rim to put your hands on

to decide where you will go and what your life will be like.
The way you now have to push yourself against the walls or furniture
to sail across the narrow room
to get close enough to the bed,
then the reaching out and grasping

hand over hand, dragging yourself
by the tightly tucked-in bedsheets.
Then the paddling against the ground with two useless feet
until you're out in the open,
where there is no leverage at all.

Seven hate poems

Hate poem 1

I hate all young people and I hate old people, and everyone who can walk and everyone with a helpful partner, I hate everyone who's not tired, everyone who lives in a house, everyone who can climb up their front steps, everyone who has doorways that can fit a wheelchair.

Hate poem 2

I hate all birthdays in the Crypt of the Undead, I hate the way the undead fold in on themselves like collapsible picnic chairs, I hate electric beds that fold me in half, nearly like a cheese sandwich but not tight enough to be a sandwich. I want my top half and bottom half to be folded together properly like a toasted sandwich, then burnt to death and spun out into the universe.

Hate poem 3

I hate the Universe so much I'm probably going to cut my wrists a little bit and bleed profusely over the Universe's linen knowing the Universe will be inconvenienced and annoyed because who likes changing bloody sheets?

Hate poem 4

I hate my brother for bringing a string of garlic into the Crypt of the Undead and telling me, *I looked for holy water and a stake but I couldn't find them.* I hate all the people who tell me: *There is light at the end of the tunnel* and *At least you didn't break your head* and *It could have been worse, you could be dead.* And *You should be grateful, imagine if you lived in the third world, stop putting your fingers in your ears and humming like that, no I won't shut up – because what I'm saying is true.*

Hate poem 5

I hate being served salmon, because I love salmon, but eating what you love in the Crypt of the Undead is total bullshit and ruins everything.

Hate poem 6

I hate visitors who feel for me and send me good vibes and prayers and blessings and love and aroha and alofa. What good is that to me? Pray for a 6-foot-7 Fijian sex worker, for fuck's sake. Let him enter this Crypt of the Undead where we can hate each other to zombie fucking death.

Hate poem 7

I hate the pain of old ladies. The things that make the pain of tiny old ladies. The turns that cause their screams. The bedsores that cause the turns that cause the screams of tiny old old ladies.

I hate the men who ask the old ladies how long it will be till they have to go to the toilet. I hate that old ladies have to guess and say, *Ten minutes.*

Mate, let me ask *you* a question: How many minutes is it till *you* have to pee?

I hate the bedpan. I hate that the old, old, tiny, tiny, lady has to ask for a lady nurse. Again. And I hate the man again. I really fucken hate that man. I hate the chainsaw thing. I hate the screaming. I hate the way the tiny, tiny, old, old lady is saying that the saw keeps cutting her and the man is calling her *ma'am* and explaining stupid shit to her while he keeps on cutting.

I hate *ma'am*. Don't anyone ever call me ma'am.

In isolation

Brown walls, damaged, weeping
Brown lamp shades, a bit like skin, a bit like lampshades
made of brown skin
Brown mirror frame, no reflection
Brown suitcase, arriving/ leaving/ going nowhere
Brown crutch, no/ body
Brown body in a white dress, no head, no arms, no legs
Brown telephone cord, old-school, unattached, that is:
our voices going nowhere.

Hotel lobby with art

The black woman is death

The three brown women in saris with snarling dogs are feminine
energy

The black woman wears killer heels/ holds a skull/ and other 'stuff'

The thing is: there is no room in the hotel for a brown woman as
feminine energy

no room for a brown woman to sink into an overflowing bubble
bath and forget about the killer dog

no room for a brown woman to ring hotel reception and ask where
the big towels are for the sauna.

The thing is: there is no place for a black woman to kick off her
killer heels, rub her aching feet and ring reception to book a foot
massage

no place for a black woman to order in an expensive dinner and ring
reception for the second time and ask whether there is a beautician

and ask/ does she do good pedicures?/ and by the way, I would like
to make a complaint to the manager/ I'm actually not okay being
listed here as death.

Big Fat Brown Bitch 56: She is sick
of writing poems no one ever reads

Men ask me on dates and say:
So, what do you do?
And I say, *I'm a writer,* which sounds a bit impressive
and a bit odd for a brown girl.
I know this cos they look kinda awestruck and hella confused.
I never say *I'm a poet,* cos $3 royalties per book
(if you've even spent 30 bucks to read this book).

I can live better than that on the benefit.
We're not poor, babe, I say to my 14-year-old daughter
when she tells me we've got to spend less on groceries
and that she doesn't have to go to the escape room with her friends
cos it's 30 bucks, which is 10 books that no one has bought.

I'm sick of writing poems no one reads.
These motherfucking poems take me years.
What a joke.
I'd rather be a school mum who talks about my renovations
and my husband and that kind of shit.

I'm sick of writing poems on one ever reads
except for middle-aged white people of a certain demographic
and smiling white-haired ladies in a line at a book signing table
and classrooms full of brown girls who are in awe of me.

My cousin says he hates poetry.
I don't blame him.
Even my own poems bore me.
Unless I'm punching someone in the face

or inveigling my invisible hand into their panties
and each stanza is making them come violently,
I'm sick of writing poems.

I'm sick of writing motherfucking poems
that no one ever reads.
This is the menopause of poetry.
The flashes of heat are over.
The sleeplessness and suicide flattened like my nipples.
Now it's the zero libido of landscape poems
and pages dry as my pussy.

I'm sick of writing poems no one ever reads.
There are countries where poets are performing to football stadiums
and the roar of prisons. Poets are being arrested and tortured
not by their own boredom but for conspiring against the government
with poems.
It's time I stopped this bullshit or lost my life trying.

4

Malu | Protection

Tualima

(for Kolotina)

My niece has decided to get the tualima// on both her hands/

Tua/ back/
Lima/ hands/
Tatau/ tattoo/

She is searching for the whakapapa/
of our symbols/
the symbols that will help her tell our story/
tell the story she is searching for/

Can you help me, Aunty?

She reminds me we have a tapa/
her great-grandmother made/
it's up in our rafters/
I have forgotten this/

Can you help me, Aunty?

I remember the tapa/
I wonder what it might say/
and how we might read it/

Above the head of my bed is a sketch of my grandmother/
the great-grandmother of my niece/
sketched by my mother/
sixty years ago// in Sāmoa/

My grandmother is weaving a fala/
it could be an ie toga/
I can't tell which/

I think about the tapa in the rafters/
and wait for my niece to come/
she wants to find her whakapapa there/

I wonder what my grandmother intended sixty years ago/
when she painted those patterns on the tapa/
perhaps they were just what looked good to her at the time/

Can you help me, Aunty, please?
(My niece wishes for so much.)

We look at my tatau books and ring the museum/
where our symbols are guarded by pālagis//
I wonder if the whakapapa of our symbols are locked away in there too/

We have to make an appointment to see them/
so we hope for the best/
we hope that whoever collected those symbols/

whatever German anthropologist (in eighteen hundred and something/
when Sāmoa belonged to him and his Kaiser)
asked someone who knew the stories/
and decided to tell the anthropologist the truth//

Aunty, who's Margaret Mead?

I smile and tell her that sometimes our ancestors
told those anthropologists all kinds of crazy stories
and laughed behind their backs.

What a egg, ay, Aunty?
Yeah, babe, what a egg.

< >

The whakapapa of a symbol

< > malu
< > at the back of a knee
< > on the back of a hand
< > a net
< > a portal
< > a protection

How do we trace the whakapapa of our symbols < > when our
grandmother is dead < > and our father is dead < > and our great
uncles and aunties are dead < >

We go to the museum

< >

When I got my tualima

I spoke to my father// dead a year
I put what he told me on paper and passed it to the first female tufuga//
since Taemā and Tilafaigā.

93

⋀ The frigate bird who flies across the seas

⋀⋀⋀⋀ to where my father lives now
      beyond the horizon

⋀ the footprint of the tern who treks
   back and forth taking messages
   to the heavens

✕ the portal between
   child and parent

◇ protected

This is the story I have told on the back of my hand.

<>

My niece and I are lost travellers

We have to find our way,
we have to search for our symbols

and pray to the marrow in our bones
for our stories,

for our whakapapa.
This is what I tell my niece.

Why don't I have a big Tongan husband or Dwayne Johnson to help me?

Vampires are always white
and here I am fighting one,
hard, like really goddamned fighting –

blood all over me,
worse than in a butcher's shop,
worse than wrestling a bleeding swine,

blood fountaining everywhere.
Someone hand me a cross, I yell
and I press it to his forehead but nothing happens.

What is this –
it's a damned spoon –
who handed me a spoon, for fuck's sake?

Hand me a stake, then!
Not a steak – don't you dare!
Why isn't my father here?
My brother?

Yeah, I'm angry, I know that.
Stop telling me how frightened I am.

The dark versus the light

Why so dark, Brown Girl, why so dark?
Be light, be lighter than light
Be light like God
Sit in a room and blast gospel music at yourself
Be lighter than God
Be the lightest possible
Sit in a room and blast *The Power of Positive Thinking* at yourself
Be white, Half-Caste Girl
You know you can do it
You are halfway there already
Be halfer that half
Be so half the other half is full of white too
Cheer up, Brown Girl
Sit in a room and blast *Mein Kampf* at yourself
and stop moaning and bitching and complaining
about racism and colonisation and white privilege
People get sick of that
It might be in fashion right now
but it won't last forever
Sit in a room and blast *The 7 Habits of Highly Effective People* at yourself
and Cheer the Fuck Up.

Malu: She has her legs tattooed 1

Whakamā: To make pure
Whakamā: To enlighten
Whakamā: To shame

<>

Sauniuniga: Preparation

Whakamā: To make pure

To protect myself with the kaupare, the chant. To erect the shield that are the words of the tangata whenua. To stand on their land and pull my father's land – from over the sea, where his bones are buried – towards myself. To swallow the rongoā, the medicine of the tangata whenua. To help me open and protect. Protect and open.

Whakamā: To enlighten

To learn the words of the lāuga, the oratory I have never known. Not in this pālagi world, not in the Samoan world either.

To hold the lāuga, the oratory, in my phone, in my eyes, in my throat and tongue and lips, in the air between my lips and all our ears. The *real* Samoan ears and the born-here ears. To memorise the sounds.

To not be able to memorise the sounds.

Whakamā: To shame

To be in the brain that does not understand the lāuga, the oratory, makes the heart beat fast and faster. Makes the skin of the face change its brown to red and the heat in the armpits wet. Makes the head lower, the pose lower. Makes the whole body smaller.

< >

The opening lāuga, the oratory

We sit
them on their side   us on ours.

Their ears understand the lāuga,
they are daughters of the bringers of the light.
They are not daughters of pālagi, no,   the half daughters
                                                                                        of pālagi are us.
The cross came. The bringers of the light came.
                                        Nafanua, the goddess of Sāmoa,
                                the goddess of peace and of war, left.
They are the brown daughters of the ones
who broke the horizon. They are the brown-
skinned daughters of the cross.   We are the light brown
                                                            daughters whose ears don't
                                                            understand the lāuga,
                                                                    the oratory.
                        We sit on opposite sides.

The goddess can look after herself. This vā, this space, is so full of Her and the underwater taniwha. Nafanua, goddess of Sāmoa, let the missionary boats set sail. She didn't haul them under the sea and swallow them. She let them come.

And here they are.   And here we are.

The afa kasis, the half-caste daughters
whose tongues are stiff
the daughters who have practised their lāuga,
their oratory, in front of their mirrors
the daughters who wrote their lāuga on cards
just in case.
The daughter who is an orator in the pālagi
language, but that is of little use today.

The daughter opens her mouth to speak the lāuga, the oratory:

*E lē galo iā tātou le mafua'aga/ o lo'o tatā ai malu a Sāmoa/ ma tatau a Sāmoa/
ona nai auso/ o Taemā ma Tilafaigā/ ma si lā Tama'ita'i toa/ o Nafanua. Mālō
le lotonaunauta'i.*

*I acknowledge and welcome the goddesses of the malu, Taemā and Tilafaigā
and their daughter the goddess Nafanua, to be with us and protect us. Help us to
honour you in receiving the malu . . .*

The daughter of the cross stands,
the daughter of the righteous
You-Shall-Have-No-Other
brown daughter of the cross stands on her side.
No godlessness in this malu space!

No Tilafaigā and Taemā:
no goddess of the malu, the tattoo.
No Nafanua:
no goddess of war and goddess of peace
No goddesses of Sāmoa
before the missionaries came.

<>

Whakamā
Fa‘amā
Whakamā

<>

Malu: She has her legs tattooed 2

The vā: The relational space between

I lie down in the vā, my face is still burning.
I lie down in the vā, the space of the half-caste,
the space of I don't know the language,

the space of mā, the space of shame.
But I lie down anyway.
I lie in the world our fathers came to from Sāmoa,

as the new ones, the ones who didn't know the language.
My father would be ninety-three years old today –
the tall man, cold, wearing his *Aloha* shirt in the slaughterhouse,

in the freezing works on the lands of Ngāti Whātua,
Ngā Oho, Wai-o-Hua.
My father returns here today.

The taniwha swim deep in the underground rivers, the lakes
that are gone now. The taniwha swim deep – big as whales, big as buses,
they swim deep and Jesus doggy-paddles on the surface.

The tanifa swim all around, big as meteors, big as stars.
I lie with the taniwha underneath me.
The mothers of the war goddess,

Tilafaigā and Taemā, who came here from the underworld
take up the ta au and the sausau.
The tufuga, the tattooist, takes up the tools and begins.

<>

Malu: She has her legs tattooed 3

Back of the right knee

Stay under the surface of the water with your eyes closed. Somewhere in the dark, stop. Open your eyes. There is enough pain to keep you under. Look up now, see the surface? The undersides of the choppy waves.

The au strikes the back of your right knee.

tap tap
tap tap

You are a sea creature now. A new one. You are a creature learning how to breathe down here. Watch the sharp waves and breathe.

tap tap
tap tap

You are not yet a mermaid or an eel or a tanifa.

Float and breathe

float and breathe.

tap tap
tap tap

Soon you will need breath no more, you will live in pain.

Back of the right thigh

This is where the witches live, the monsters, the taniwha without faces. This is where they live and you don't have a choice –

be drowned

be drowned here.

Upper side of the right thigh

This is where the whirlpool is. No one will tell you until you are deep in the funeral, you are deep in the grave and you are mourning.

You are your own keener –

Aueeeeeeeeeeeeeeeeeeeeeeeeee

Auoiiiiiiiiiiiiiiiiiiiiiiiiiiiiiiiiiiiiiiiiiiiiiiiiiiiiiiiiiiiiiiiiiii

Aueeeeeeeeeeeeeeeeeeeeeeeeeeeeeeeeeeeeeee

Inside of the right thigh

No time for crying now. This is when we tie one leg to the taniwha who is a bus, the other leg to a tanifa who is called ride-'em-cowboy.

This is where we pull you apart to see what is inside you.

Back of the left knee

It has gone before you knew you were there.

All the taniwha in the room, the light-brown half-caste tanifa. All the taulāsea, the light-brown girls with the ancestors growing out of the palms of their hands gather for the back of the left thigh. This is when they lay the palms of their hands on you and the Christians approve because laying on of hands is in the Bible.

The taniwha eat small fish and small people who dog paddle at the surface. Let them sharpen their teeth on you first. They will sharpen, so let them. Throw your arms out as if you are being crucified and say

Yes, Jesus, sharpen your teeth on me now

tap tap
tap tap

Inside of the left thigh

Open the inside of your left thigh to Jesus – Jesus, come and eat me now. I am Jesus Vagina dentata, Hine-nui-te-pō and that outta-luck guy Māui.

tap tap
tap tap

Eat me like a cannibal, like a savage, like the blood and the body and the thorn-crown, thrown together in a twisted heap onto the backyard lawn.

Eat me like an old-school hand-pushed mower with blades sharp as Hades-Hell-and-Pulotu.

Front of the left knee

This is the final shredding. Sharpen your blade on the front of my left knee –

tap tap
tap tap

Drill for oil and gold and petroleum. Drill for gemstone, limestone, kidneystone and rock salt. Drill for heartland, brokenheart, chickenheart and lonelyheart.

Bend my leg to a tent and pound the bones of my knee: patella, femur, fibula and the in-between meniscus. Chip and carve like all the Renaissance sculptors and their hammers, like all the angry 1970s secretaries and their typewriters.

tap tap
tap tap

Bang out the letters hard and fast now, till all the keys tangle and snap. Let them land like stars creating their own maps.

<>

Malu: She has her legs tattooed 4

Samaga, closing ceremony

You stand in front of your family and friends with your lavalava hiked up high so everyone can behold the new creature

You cross over to sit on your side with your women and wait

Closing oratory, lāuga reboot

The Christian Samoan sits across from you and says things you strain to understand

Now it's your turn to speak – this is what you think she says – so you open your mouth

You thank God this time (yes, the Christian one) to be in front of the house where good luck lives and not in the back with the – and she cuts you off again, in the middle of your lāuga, your oratory, *again*

No, she says, *you got it wrong.*

Whakamā: to shame

Enlightenment comes as shame

The hot burn

The hot hot burn

The *stupid half-caste can't speak Samoan bloody New Zealand-born why don't you go back to your own country*

Enlightenment comes as shame

Mā

Maaaa

Maaaaaaaaaaaaaaaaaaaaaaaaa

Whakamā: to whiten, to make pure, to enlighten

The egg is cracked over your head

The symbolism dribbles down your face and hangs from your nostrils

You decide to say the rest of your oratory in English –

even the expert fisherman makes mistakes –

The waves of shame break

to cleanse you

to cleanse you.

<>

Glossary

<> a version of malu symbol for protection

afa kasi: half caste

fala: woven mat for everyday use

Hawaiki Nui: ancient Polynesian homeland

Hine-nui-te-pō: goddess of death and the underworld

ie toga: woven fine mat for ceremonial use

ifoga: traditional Samoan apology ceremony

ika: fish

kaikaranga: woman who makes the ceremonial call

karanga mai ra: welcome chant

lāuga: oratory

lavalava: Samoan wraparound; sarong

malu: protection

malu: traditional Samoan women's tattoo, from upper thigh to lower knee

manawa: heart

Māui: demigod trickster

Nafanua: Samoan war goddess

nifo koula: gold tooth

Oi Manawa: Canterbury Earthquake National Memorial

pālagi: white person (pā: to break; lagi: sky – reference to the goddess Nafanua's prophecy that the pālagi would come to Sāmoa)

Papatūānuku: goddess of the earth

shuhada: martyr

siapo: see 'tapa'

susu: breasts

ta au, sausau: Samoan tattoo tools

Taemā and Tilafaigā: twin goddesses who brought the art of tatau/tattoo from Fiji to Sāmoa. Tilafaigā was Nafanua's mother.

tanifa: supernatural sea creature

taniwha: supernatural creature that often lives in or near water

tapa: Pasifika bark cloth

taulāsea: Samoan traditional healer

tualima: Samoan women's tattoo – back of hand

tufuga: master tattooist

vā: Samoan concept of relational space

whakapapa: line of descent

Notes

p. 11: Text from 'Poet Tusiata Avia lashes ACT after party calls book The Savage Coloniser "racist" and "hate-fuelled"', *Newshub*, 2 March 2023. Photo illustration based on composite image from 'Media Council tosses out complaints about Tusiata Avia The Savage Coloniser poem published on Stuff', *Newshub*, 14 April 2023.

Free speech poem, p.13: The un-redacted poem, '250th anniversary of James Cook's arrival in New Zealand', appears in *The Savage Coloniser Book* (Victoria University Press, 2020).

New Zealand Media Council Complaints Case 3392, p. 16: This poem includes direct quotes from complainants in the New Zealand Media Council report, case 3392.

Hey David, p. 21: This poem is a response to the news stories referenced above.

And for their next trick, p. 24: This poem contains a reference to 'Song of Myself' (51) by Walt Whitman, *Leaves of Grass* (Norton, 1973).

Diary of a death threat, 15 March 2023 (Anniversary), p. 28: 15 March 2023 was the four-year anniversary of the Christchurch mosque shootings.

Glorious ways rap, p. 41: This poem borrows its first line from Morgan Parker's poem 'The World Is Beautiful But You Are Not In It', from *Other People's Comfort Keeps Me Up At Night* (Switchback Books 2015; Tin House 2021). It is also inspired by the song 'Not Many' by Scribe. There are references to Matthew 7:5, 13–14.

Ode: Don't punish the wealthy, p. 44: This poem is a response to comments made by Nicola Willis in her speech, 'Fixing the Economy', to the 87th National Party conference, 24 June 2023.

Dawn Raids Apology 2022, p. 47: One of the tactics that police used during the Dawn Raids was to play recordings of dogs barking on loudspeakers, to drive overstayers out of their hiding places. A counter technique by the Polynesian Panthers was to 'raid' MPs' houses before dawn with bright lights and loud hailers.

Another England built, p. 66: This poem refers to the following news stories. 'Man arrested after allegedly stabbing woman in Christchurch', *Stuff*, 23 November 2022; 'Two people charged after Chistchurch dog walker stabbed repeatedly', *Stuff*, 11 November 2023.

Big Fat Brown Bitch 66: She performs an exorcism, p. 68: This poem responds to the following article: 'White supremacist Philip Arps standing for school board prompts call for rule change', RNZ, 16 August 2022.

Malu: She has her legs tattooed 4, p. 106: This poem makes reference to several Samoan proverbs, including 'E poto le tautai ae se le atu i ama' ('Even the expert fisherman makes mistakes').

Thank you | Fa'afetai lava

To my gafa | whakapapa who hold me: Namulau'ulu Mikaio, Catherine Sylvia and Sepela Catherine Tali'ilagi and the long line who follow

Ashleigh Young for her patient help and good humour with editing

Fergus Barrowman and Te Herenga Waka University Press for putting this book out into the world, which marks (nearly) twenty years of publishing together

Nurses and carers at Christchurch Hospital and Essie Summers Retirement Village, where I spent three months recovering from an accident and writing some of this book – a weird, enforced writer's residency

My friends and family who visited me during those three months and brought me beautiful skin products, coffee, and their company

Hinemoana Baker for letting me use some of her words in 'Seven hate poems (Hate poem 3)' and for keeping me sane in my darkest time in hospital

The cast and crew of *The Savage Coloniser Show* for giving some of these poems life onstage

Auckland Arts Festival for giving me security guards during the show

Big alofa and gratitude to those in the writing community who supported and defended me when my name was dragged through the media mud. I was in social media lockdown to avoid hate mail and sadly I missed messages of support too, but I know a number of you had my back – fa'afetai tele lava

Sherry Zhang at *The Pantograph Punch*, Sam Ackerman at *The Big Idea* and Susana Leiataua at RNZ, who gave me a platform when the storm was raging

Claire Mabey for writing an excellent guide to reading the poem that made everyone so crazy and to thinking about our own colonisation and racism: 'How to read a poem', *The Spinoff*, 27 February 2023

My malu sisters/siblings: my soa, Carlene Kelso; my daughter, Sepela; Aunty Leitu'u, cousins and dear friends who sat with me during my malu

Maria Lemalie for coming to my aid at the last minute with my manuscript

Selina for reminding me to listen to myself

And the hate-fuelled racists: those in the ACT Party, Seymour and van Velden; to Willis, Luxon and Winston; to Plunket and the ever more creepy, less visible creatures of the internet – you continue to inspire me.

Encore: The Big Fat Brown Bitch Sings The Savage Pussy Song

This is the Big Fat Brown Bitch song
The brown girl savage song
We're gonna fuck you with our song
With the Big Fat Brown Girl song

Captain Cook was so wrong
when he came here on the rough seas
This is the brown girl savage song
Y'all are racist fragile flunkies

We're not good girls, we're not twiggy
We are big, fat, bad and pretty
We don't really wanna stab you
You know that and we damn you

Winston, David, Sean and Nobby
You guys are really creepy
Captain Cook and all the shooters
Y'all people are the looters

Yo, Mr Luxon you're so wrong
Your racist Southside song
Your garage of disparage
We're gonna fuck you with our song.

This is the Big Fat Brown Bitch song
The savage pussy song
We're gonna fuck you with our song
With the savage pussy song.